Publisher Info

D1527341

Welcome! And enjoy just a few key lessons that I've learned not only playing poker, but in life. They've helped me stay positive and motivated when I'm winning, losing...and all the times in between.

Table Of Contents

Imagine Your Winning Possibilities

01

Get Where You Want to Be

Hard Question

How do you get to where you want to be in life? What does it take to be the President? Or for you to become the most valuable player on a team? How about a highly paid professional?

How do you reach your desired goals in life? You must be ready to learn how to walk on water, to walk across red-hot coals, to dare go where your dreams will take you.

It isn't always easy

I welcome everyone to imagine great possibilities. To achieve your goals in life, you must believe all things are possible, all goals are achievable, if you are truly focused, prepared, and trained. That focus comes from having clarity and knowing what you want to achieve. That's when you can clearly see your goals at the end of tunnel.

All victories in achieving goals require preparation. When you practice, rehearse, train, and perform those activities necessary to achieve your goals, then you are on the right path.

Enjoy life's detours

Sometimes when traveling this path towards your goals, you may have unforeseen obstacles along the way. These obstacles often cause detours. Don't see this as a negative! Instead, learn to enjoy the scenery while on your detour.

On a detour you can make many friends and acquire new skills along your journey. During this time being off your path, you will often gain your greatest insights, and enhance your strength and your determination.

Finding inspiration

Many people have had to move off the pathway towards their life's goals.

Muhammad Ali, the 20th-century professional fighter, was on the road to becoming the "Heavyweight Champion of the World" but had to detour, thanks to the Draft Board during the Vietnam War.

Thanks to racial bias that put him in prison for 27 years, Nelson Mandela of Africa went on a long detour before becoming the President of South Africa.

I myself was on my way to becoming a highly paid IT professional when I had a detour caused by the United States Army. But it was there I learned new skills and met new friends.

The power of Faith

While being off your desired path, you will realize that it is the hunger for your goals that will put you back on the right path. Your journey may be long, you may even become lost at some point, even lose your determination. In these moments of desperation, it is essential to have a leap of faith.

Faith is the power within your heart, deep down in your soul, the place where your being starts, and dreams are borne. Faith is what it takes to do the impossible.

It will be this Faith that will take you beyond your perceived limits, beyond your current strength. It is by this Faith that you will learn to move beyond your biggest dreams. It is why you will dare to go where your dreams will take you.

Faith is how you get where you want to be and reach your goals in life, be it in poker or anything else.

Keep the Faith!

02

Educated in Iowa

I was born in Baltimore, Maryland, in a row house on Fulton and North Avenue. But I attended the Iowa State University Graduate School for Computer Science in the Fall of 1976. At that point, I had never been west of Virginia in my whole life.

You may ask, how in the world did this odd event occur? Many people both in Baltimore and Iowa asked this question all the time.

It was totally unplanned and—born and raised as a big city dweller—I admit I had no desires to go to Iowa.

It was a tough start

It all started 1973 in my sophomore year at Morgan State University, a traditional Black school in Northeast Baltimore. There were a small number of White students, whose main reason for attending was the fact that they received a full scholarship from the school to meet a racial quota required by the government.

I was so poor that at Morgan State I used to sit in the cafeteria drinking sugar water because the sugar bags were free. All the money that I had went towards my tuition, so many times, I sat in the cafeteria starving, drinking my sugar water and wondering, "Where could I get paid to go to school?" But I had no idea.

It pays to explore every option

One day on campus there was an Open House for recruiting students to graduate schools. I went to the open house and saw over 50 different schools being represented. As I walked thru the gym, I noticed that all the large East and West Coast schools were filled with curious students looking for information.

Then I noticed one table with a lonely guy attracting no students. The sign on his table was labeled, "Iowa State University Graduate School." I decided to walk over and give him a hard time about why no one was at his table. He just smiled and said that they had great schools, great programs, and great teachers.

He was giving me a brochure as I was leaving, but right before I got out of hearing distance, he added, "And they will pay you to come."

I froze in my steps. I could not believe what I'd just heard. Immediately, I went back to the table. I told him I wanted to go to a computer science graduate school and he said theirs was great; they would give me a job, a room on campus, and pay the tuition.

Ahhh...just one catch

I was very happy until he asked, "What is your grade point average?" After my answer he said, "You know they don't give scholarships to students with a 2.5 GPA."

So I started to leave again—and then he said more magic words: "If you get your GPA to up 3.0, I promise I will get you a scholarship."

"Yes, I can do it!" I replied.

It was a changing point in my college career. I went from a slacker with no sense of direction to a totally focused, goal-oriented student. I did my homework, term papers, studies, and the most unbelievable action of all: telling friends on Friday nights that I must study instead of partying. (I lost friends, BTW.)

In my senior year, I had a 3.3 GPA and received an acceptance notice to Iowa State University's graduate program. I was very excited...until I told my family I was going to college in Ames, Iowa.

Imagine Your Winning Possibilities

Where did you say you're going?

My mother always knew that I was special. Still, neither she nor my other family members had ever heard of, or even knew the location of, Iowa State University. You should have seen my mom's face when I got the atlas out and pointed to the middle of the country, then to Iowa, then to Ames in the middle of Iowa.

She asked, "Why in the world are you going there?" I looked up and said, "Because this is the opportunity of a lifetime."

Exploring a new world

In the fall of 1976, I was on a Greyhound bus heading to Iowa. Two days later—after seeing every bus stop between Baltimore and Ames, Iowa!—I arrived at Iowa State University (ISU).

After checking in to the graduate dormitory, I met my new roommate, Chen Chong from China. He was an engineering student. We got along great, though he could not understand some of my American ways of partying and bringing girls to the room. I think this was the reason why on Spring break he flew home and got married.

One day between classes, I spent an hour watching thousands of students walking across campus. That's when I realized that America is White. ISU's population of about 24,000 students has about a 0.5 percent Black student population. You know what this meant? When you met another Black student you always had long conversations.

On campus, one of the most common questions people often asked me was, "What sport do you play? I always looked them straight in the eye and responded, "Basketball center guard."

One day when I went shopping at the food store right off campus, there was this small White kid and his mother shopping. The kid grabbed his mother's arm and said, "Look mommy! There is Fat Albert." I totally understood the kid because in Iowa TV was the only place he'd seen a Black man.

I think living eight years in Iowa without any racial issues or incidents was because Iowa never had many Black people living there, and so maybe it didn't build generations of racism.

A little extra education

After graduate school, I worked in downtown Des Moines, Iowa. I could go for six months without talking to a Black person. I even had to come home to get a haircut.

Also, I learned that, to Iowans, 10 degrees is just "a little chilly" day. That's because the four seasons are almost winter, winter, still winter...and road construction.

And unlike in Baltimore, some folks have more hours on their lawn mowers and snow blowers than miles on their cars.

Still, being educated in Iowa taught me two things besides computer skills: First, that people are pretty much the same everywhere.

And second, if you want a good education—be it in getting more poker-playing or other skills, distance should be of no concern; you just must be willing to travel.

A COMFORT ZONE IS A BEAUTIFUL PLACE BUT NOTHING EVER GROWS THERE

03

My 2020 Vision

I will always remember the year 2020 by the good and bad experiences I had living in quarantine. The locked-down living only gave me insider jokes, like "Why did the chicken cross the road?" The best answer: "He wanted to social distance."

My overall worst vision was seeing how the most powerful person in the world generated stupidity, with statements like saying drinking bleach might kill the virus inside of you! Of course, since you can't fix stupidity, there were some folks out there who followed this advice. That's why so many leaders urged Americans to only listen to true scientists.

Creating new perspectives

Some of the bad experiences I had in 2020 forced me to reprogram some values that I'd learned over the years.

For example:
"Being a positive person is no longer a good thing. To be truly loved and valued, you must now be a negative person."

Another example:
"Paying bills on time was a good value...until I paid in cash last January for my boat cruise not happening 'til June, and I paid my dentist in February for a crown that wouldn't be installed 'til April."

Honorably paying on time made both of these payments a waste of money, at least initially. I finally either got refunds or dollars off service later on, but it was initially a negative to lose this money.

Appreciating seemingly small good changes

Now for the good visions that I keep remembering, even after the year 2020. For example:
"The day my boss told me to stay at home and work there, because it was the best place to do my work as a professional IT specialist."

In fact, my greatest workday all year was when I made overtime pay while working from my bed!

This was my best work achievement all year and it gave me a new look not only at work values, but also figuring out my best ways to work. I no longer dread going into the office, but I enjoy staying in bed thanks to building my office on my nightstand. Indeed, I've learned so well to work smarter—not harder— in bed that I keep softer pillows around me...because I could be there all day.

One of my most rewarding visions came from seeing myself in line 5:00 a.m. on a Saturday morning at my local Giant supermarket. Holding 12 rolls of toilet paper, I beat out 30 people running to the paperware aisle.

Here are a few more examples I never saw coming:

- Being at the bank and the manager welcomes in masked people, but not allowing unmasked people to enter the door. (Nor did I see my kids yelling at me for going outside of the house and questioning me on where I was going!)
- A liquor store delivery person leaving my order at my front door...with only a one- hour wait!
- A UPS driver dropping off the box of wine from California that I'd ordered online only a week earlier.

And just when I thought that there could be no more good experiences, I checked my bank account and saw the United States government depositing $1200—my stimulus check—in my checking account without any paperwork.

Yes, I will always remember my good and bad experiences in the year 2020. So to help keep a positive poker mindset, remember and learn from all your experiences, good or bad.

04

The Art of Doing Nothing

Thanks to my great dedication to working hard, I have finally achieved the power to relax on demand, to eliminate stress in life, prevent depression...even enjoy playing poker.

It wasn't easy. I admit it took me many years in my onsite federal government career—and two years of working from home during the pandemic—to learn what I call "The Art of Doing Nothing."

It's a skill that many people don't understand and never value. The only time they seem to recognize it is when they can yell at performers, "You are doing nothing!"

Many others learn this art only after spending thousands of dollars and years of practice. But I learned it for free, thanks to a different kind of practice and hard training.

The dangerous goal

The biggest reasons why people have stress, high blood pressure, and depression is because they are doing too much, working too much, and trying to achieve too much. These are your big planners, over-achievers, and must-do-it-now types of people. They never rest until the job is done. This group of highly motivated go-getters will almost always be found at the highest levels of all jobs.

Sounds great, right? But because they can't turn off their phone, get off the computer, or stop hustling for money, they will always be on their business clock 24 hours a day, seven days a week.

And this means they will never have time to smell the roses, listen to the birds, and just live a good life.

Defining a different kind of good life

Most people say truly working is hard, while playing poker makes you look lazy. But refining the "Art of Doing Nothing" can be hard to do...even though it can look like you are lazy. It really falls right between work and play. Once you do refine the almost lost "Art of Doing Nothing," you gain a host of great physical and mental health benefits, including:

- Decreased blood pressure
- Boosted memory
- Sparked creativity
- Fighting depression
- More relaxation
- Increased sense of well-being
- Reduced stress

Surprisingly easy tactics, but hard to start

The activities used to achieve this skill take only 5 to 10 minutes each day in a quiet place. Whether you find that spot at home or outdoors—or even at work—research shows a variety of ways you can relax.

For example:

- Sit or lie down, then take deep calming breaths
- Take a warm bath or shower
- Listen to nature's sounds (real or recorded) like flowing water, birds singing, or softly playing certain classical music
- Read a good book
- Walk and smell roses and other Botanics
- Lie outside and look at the clouds

It all looks easy, right? But remember this: while you can appear to be doing nothing, you are creating active relaxation. This Art of Doing Nothing will allow you to connect to your inner self have a healthier life, and develop a better poker game.

It's a mindset (and activity!) I highly recommend.

05

Why Does a Smart Man Go Broke?

Most men dream about their future and setting goals to achieve a life dream. A common goal is retiring with plenty of money. But how smart is it to struggle to save?

That common goal

There are people working hard each day to pay their bills and save some money for their retirements. Work becomes a seemingly virtuous cycle of getting up, going to work day after day, and then coming home. And that's it.

It's so bad it seems that you visit your home for a few hours each day, then you go back to the place you "really" live: work. not only live at work, they have work wives, husbands...even families. The people on your job know more about your life then your actual family. You can look at your desk and see years of history from the pictures, certificates, and awards. This is the American way of life.

Breaking the cycle

I recognize this cycle of "I've got to go to work". We all tend to develop this cycle as our means to achieve our life dreams. After all, a very wise man once said, "All work and no play makes me dull all day."

I chose to break the destructive work cycle by taking a day off in the middle of the week. Thus, I created a personal holiday known as a "Breakcation." It's any time off from work; it may also be known as a sick day or vacation day.

My pattern starts by leaving my home in the Baltimore area of Maryland at about 7:30 a.m. and taking a bus to Atlantic City, NJ. Surprisingly, at this early morning time, you will find many people in the parking lot waiting for the casino bus, mostly retired seniors. It's undoubtedly because they not only have the time, but 'cause the bus ride is almost free; the casinos will give you half your costs in slot dollars and the other half in food vouchers.

I learned early on that as people get on these bus rides, you can see in their eyes an almost magical question: "Is this my lucky day?" But I quickly decided as I got on the bus to always ask a second part to that question: "And how much will it cost me to find out?"

What's wrong with this picture?

Starting at age 35, I was usually the youngest on the bus. And by my second or third trip I realized that of around 52 passengers I was one of maybe only four or five guys.

Then I also realized that the rest of folks around me—mostly little old ladies—were generally telling stories sharing a common theme: "Their poor husbands all worked themselves to death." So all these ladies were going to Atlantic City to gamble away their dead husbands' life Insurance and other "smart" savings!

And this led me to a special insight: "A 'Smart' Man Goes Broke Without Gambling".

The smart man's budget plan

How does a traditional "smart man" go broke? At retirement, they pay off all of their major bills, and then follow what seems like an intelligent strategy.

Let's say you retire at the age of 66, and figure on living to age 78, the average American male lifespan. Next, add up all of your life savings for a grand total and divide it by those remaining 12 years.

The resulting total, minus taxes and paying major bills, shows the amount a smart man figures he can spend monthly each year.

And this led me to a special insight: "A 'Smart' Man Goes Broke Without Gambling."

Here's some math

For example, let's say you had a savings of $400,000. First you smartly put aside 20% for taxes. That leaves $ 320,000. Now let's say you had $100,000 in major bills; once you pay those off that leaves $220,000. Then you take the $220,000 and divide it by 12—the years in your remaining lifespan--and you get $18,333.

This means you figure you'll be able to spend $18,333 each year for the next 12 years. It also includes a very important conclusion: that your day-to-day expenses will be paid from your pension and Social Security checks.

So If you're lucky, you'll have a dozen golden years to spend your $220,000---and then go broke. (Oh...and yes, "smart" women can follow essentially the same process... just add in a few more years.)

Setting a different bet

My bus rides enlightened me to this reality and what changed my mindset. It's why I didn't just start figuring out what I wanted my monthly retirement savings to give me. I realized I'd have to ask myself, "How much more are you setting aside— now and later—for betting?"

And that's the ultimate question you need to ask yourself. What is the nest egg you want? Is it totally so kids or others will have dollars to inherit? Or is it so you can start building your poker lifestyle ASAP?

If it's for moving onto that lifestyle, then start planning immediately. How much can you wisely cut from monthly income now to create a successful poker-playing strategy? And what else do you need to understand to put together a true plan? The answers to that last question is what this book is about.

06

Choosing To Be Happy

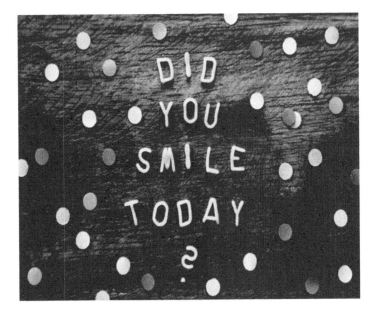

Did you know happiness is a choice made each day? When you choose love, moving forward, doing the right thing, believing in your own thoughts, and controlling your emotions, then your choice is Happiness. That means today, right now, you need to choose the Happy Path.

Why should you choose the Happy Path?

Improving your life with a goal towards being happy will bring you less stress, better relationships, more life quality, and overall better health.

It's important to remember every day that there's a reason for the old saying, "Money cannot buy happiness." The richest people are not always happy. The poorest people are not always sad. So don't think that playing poker—even winning—will always keep you happy.

Making choices

If you are sad today, then you made poor choices in the past. But you can move forward, towards happiness, by choosing loving not hating, moving forward not backwards.

Happiness means choosing right not wrong, choosing self-esteem not self-pity. And it means choosing to listen to your own thoughts, not the opinions of other people.

All this means you must practice controlling your emotions and not letting other people determine your mood and feelings. When you keep hope, confidence, and positive optimism, then you will stay on the Happy Path in life.

Enjoying that Happy Path

If you are happy today, then you have chosen wisely in the past.

The best way to stay on the Happy Path is to focus on the moment; be in the now, here in the present. When you learn to enjoy the beauty around you, you will realize, "I can choose to be happy".

And when you learn to stop judging and finding faults in other people, and learn that each person is on their own chosen path at this moment, then you will understand, "I have the power within myself at any given moment to uplift my emotions, to stay positive, to be inspired and to feel good now."

Staying on your Happy Path

What are the biggest requirements for staying on your Happy Path? It's having gratitude, keeping healthy relationships, practicing self-love, and making good choices in life.

It's also important to remember that it is hard to stay on the Happy Path because you will always have obstacles on your poker-playing path, obstacles that cause setbacks and emotional stress.

But if you are not happy at any moment, you can stay happy even during the stresses we all feel while on your poker-playing path.

Just remember this:

"Happiness is a choice you make every day."

07

Becoming Legendary

This quote motivates me:

"I used to think being good was enough, until I learned that I could be great. Today, I realize, I can choose to be Legendary!"

If you refer to someone as "Legendary," you might mean that they are very famous and admired by many people. But you can also mean a "legend" is someone of extraordinary accomplishment.

Imagine yourself to be the type of person you want to be. Imagine you have everything you wanted in life.

Imagine you have all the fame and glory you desired. If you had all of this, then you would be legendary.

I found a path to reach this goal. It's through poker.

Start with simple measures

Why poker, you may ask? Why would that make me (or anyone) legendary? Because all of us can start playing without any special college degree, official license, permit, or permission from any authorities.

Because poker puts us in charge of our own success. Like me, your performance, your decisions, and your determination, help you achieve that success.

You can measure your poker-playing success at any point in time. You can add up all the money you won playing poker and compare it to all the money you lost playing poker. A total above zero means that you are successful, and on your way toward your goal. If the total is below zero, then you need more practice, more discipline, and more determination. You must never give up, for it is only in trying and persisting that dreams come true.

Dreaming really big

My ultimate dream: Go to Las Vegas and play in the World Series of Poker (WSOP) Main Event to win 10 million dollars.

The biggest dream stopper: the $10,000 cost to enter.

Who in the world would pay $10,000 to play a game of cards against thousands of people who have and treat $10,000 like loose change?

I know who. It's a person like me.

You need to be a person who says, "I have possibilities." A person who thinks, "One can only do impossible things, if they believe in impossible things". A person who can imagine himself (or herself) as a great poker player and then goes on to become one.

Finding a dream path

I learned that the casino I chose had a tournament contest that would give you the $10,000 for a seat at the WSOP Main Event in Las Vegas.

In January 2019, I entered the tournament and paid the entry fee. At the tournament, I later learned that another 100 people also had the same idea and dream to win the seat.

I did not even make it to the first tournament break before I was knocked out of it.

A different kind of bravery

Winston Churchill once said, "It is the courage to continue that counts." And that's not only a matter of facing true military battles...it's any of life's challenges.

This was the reason why I tried again in February. Again, I did not make it to the first break before I was knocked out.

But—learning that only in trying and persisting do dreams come true—I played again in March. This time I made it past the first break...and then I was knocked out!

In April, I entered the contest again. Not only did I know that I had possibilities, I knew the more I played, the more I persisted, the more I showed up, the more I would be prepared for victory.

This time I made it past the first break. Then past the second break. And even past the third break. I got to the Final Table!

The next thing I knew, I became the last man standing. I had that $10,000 seat at WSOP. I beat out 126 people fighting for the ticket!

In conclusion, you must follow your dreams. Dare go to the places your dreams will take you. You must persist and not be deterred if you want to reach those dreams. I learned that in life, I can not only be great...one day I can be truly legendary.

About Your Author

As you've already read, "Mr. Possibilities," has had life experiences in poker and beyond.

He started in a lower-income--but very loving home--in Maryland, and originally wasn't that great a student--or poker player! Like lots of folks, his grades weren't originally that good and his very tight budget made shouldering college expenses a burden. So much so, that quite honestly he was doing far more partying than studying.

But a great opportunity arose...and it's seeing opportunities that help all of us rise in any career, including poker. Mr. Possibilities used his opportunity to get a college degree in IT and it was that which led to learning poker.

It's because he had a steady income and found ways to take time off and go to a well-run gambling operation: the casinos in Atlantic City.

The rest, as they say, is history. It's about how to take that time off and mindsets you need to keep succeeding, whether you go at poker for some part-time income or (now that Mr. Possibilities' retired) for more full-time work.

Trust this inspires you in poker and perhaps even other areas.

Please write a
motivational book review
Thank you,
Mr. Possibilities. :-)

Please visit my Book List Website for Low Content books like Logbooks, Sign-in/ Sign-out books, and guest books: https://maidenmadellc.com/

Made in the USA
Middletown, DE
23 September 2023

39140858R00027